IN HIS LIGHT

Dorian Petersen Potter

IN HIS LIGHT

I want to dedicate this poetry book to God, and to Jesus Christ,
my Lord and my Savior. They had always been in my life
the biggest and greatest inspiration of all.
Thank You God and Jesus for all that You both had
done, and for your most wonderful gift of
love, forgiveness and salvation.

SAVIOR

(Pantoum)

Because You're our Savior and King
Let's unite our voices in praise
When I think of You my heart sing
Lord help me walk in your will, ways.

Let's unite our voices in praise
To world proclaim all Your glory
Lord help me walk in Your will, ways
In You have greatest love story.

To world proclaim all Your glory
When I think of You my heart sing
In You have greatest love story
Because You're our Savior and King.

~Forgive~

(Pantoum)

When folks are mean, just let it go
In silence forgive, then move on
Sometimes is best to go with flow
Anger brings pain none good to show.

In silence forgive, then move on
Not easy, but right thing to do
Anger brings pain none good to show
Allow no one make your day just blue.

Not easy, but right thing to do
Sometimes is best to go with flow
Allow no one turn your day just blue
When folks are mean, just let it go.

~From You Lord~

(The Tree)

From
You Lord
Gain my strength
I trust in You
With You have a home
In your love truly glow
To you I come in prayer
Help me every day not to stray
F
R
O
M
YOU LORD.

*
*
*

~His Perfect Plan~

(Tree of Life)

God
Uplift
My spirit
It's under fire
I ask for your help
Oh Lord please protect me
Help soul and mind forever
Enemy likes to hurt each day
I pray to you and call your name
Foe brings sorrow and wants to steal my peace
I pray to you help me God and protect me
On You rests all my forgiveness and salvation
Guide me with your hand help me see everything better
I know the sky
Is the limit
Help me always
Not be afraid
You show The Way
Have perfect plan

~He's In All That's Great and Good~

(Eleventh Power)

When I wake up enjoy what I can today
In worship spend time with God thank Him for all
He gives plenty of blessings to me and you
Praise Him all the time and seek him when I fall
Feel his love today and try walk in his way
He'll protect you always you don't have to crawl
When we put God first in all we will just grow
Under his loving care then our souls will glow
Just have faith and stand in Jesus tall and strong
Devil try block way and bring you only wrong
But with God you defeat devil and sing songs.

~Only God Knows That~

(Monologue Style)

God knows what's in
your heart you know that
He's giving you so
many beautiful
things and much more
You can cheat and be
deceitful and steal and tell lies but

To God you can't
never just deceive
no matter what
you do or may try
He knows what's in
mind, you can't outsmart
Because only God really knows heart.

~With Him I Can Cope~

(Christ-In-A-Rhyme)

Some folks losing their health and sleep
They need jobs to eat, home to keep
For their family they care deep

Times always change and so many things go wrong or move slow
Food prices just rise high and finances and spirits get low
Folks one by one lose their hopes and dreams when no more there's flow

Folks can't find job they get sad
Some things can get very bad
So much pain many get mad

Life can get so hard
It plays good bad cards
Takes us all off guard

But with God can hope
Smile and not just mope
With Him I can cope.

~By His Power~

(Sexain poem)

Sin is sin despite topic or size in God's eyes
God tells us of this in his Holy Book you see
There's no such thing as small or big sin
God hates sin but no sinners or anything akin
He created the world perfect a long time ago
It was paradise, till Adam and Eve fell you know.

It was great till Satan tempted them and both fell
Right after that happened nothing went for them well
Satan told them a big lie and both fell for it
Disobedience against God greatest mistake made every bit.
That was the day that sin entered this world first time
We're product of sin, but with Jesus we can clean all the grime.

~A Peaceful Glow~

(Unmetered Quatrain)

No matter what your troubles
From Him feel that peaceful glow
Sometimes troubles comes in doubles
For reasons we don't know

So keep a door always open
No matter what your cares
In case you need to re-open
Each and all your dares

Take the time now to enter
There's much we want to share
Always make God and love the center
Of all your attention if you really care!

The love will surely flow
Come and share your life the hours
Here love will always glow
And bring you within more power!

So come inside and rest a while
No matter what your cares
Keep on your face an open smile
Love in your heart always wear.

~Courage~

(Quatrains)

Day by day I've seen you
With courage fight your way through
You never quit and you're so strong
As you press your way ahead no matter what's wrong.

You continue in your mind with a song all along
You always set your goals where you know they belong
And in your heart you try to follow well His plan
That you can do it, and I just know that you really can.

I know that you have a bunch on your plate, in your mind
But no matter what's around you, or bad, you're always kind
So many losses in your life you've already gone thru, so much pain
But through all, I know that God and your faith has kept you sane.

~His Peace~

(Carpe Diem)

Things you said are not yet a fact

Thinking it not an act

But still broke heart

Apart

You're young, vulnerable and perhaps confused

I'm stressed

Hard just to think

Spirit low I just sink

Still God in this will see me through

And will hold us strong, bring peace to us too.

~PRAYING FOR YOU~

(QUATRAIN)

I AM PRAYING FOR YOU
YOU HAVE PAIN AND SORROWS
BUT IN CHRIST THERE'S TOMORROW
HE IS RIGHT THERE WITH YOU.

TRUST HIM AND TEST HIS WAYS
HE WON'T LEAVE YOU ALONE
HIS MERCY WILL BE SHOWN
WHEN ON HIS LIGHT YOU STAY.

NOW MY HEART BLEEDS FOR YOU
HOPING YOU FIND YOUR WAY
DAILY TO THE LORD PRAY
HELP YOU WITH BLUES TODAY.

AROUND~

(CARPE DIEM)

HAVE FAITH AND TURN YOUR WAY AROUND

LET GOD LEND YOU A HAND

JUST THINK POSITIVE

GOD CARES

DON'T LET ANYTHING DESTROY ALL YOUR DREAMS

STAND STRONG

SEEK LORD TODAY

PRAY HIM AND FIND HIS WAY

GIVE HIM THANKS FOR ALL HIS BLESSINGS

SPEND TIME WITH HIM THIS DAY AND EVERY DAY.

~WITH JESUS I CAN~

(QUATRAIN)

WITH JESUS YOU CAN ATTAIN ALL
PICK YOU UP EVERY TIME YOU FALL
HE REINFORCES GOOD THAT YOU KNOW
AND GOES EVERYWHERE THAT YOU GO.

WITH GOD YOU CAN ENDURE LONG
KNOWING HE'S NEAR MAKE YOU STRONG
WHEN IN NEED JUST SAY A PRAYER
WALKING WITH HIM ALL I CAN BEAR.

WITH GOD I DON'T REALLY HAVE TO CRAWL
WITH MY LORD JESUS I CAN HAVE IT ALL
THINKING ABOUT HIM MAKES SOUL SOAR HIGH
PLEASING HIM MAKES MY HEART VERY HAPPY.

~NO MATTER WHAT HE CARES FOR ME~

(RONDEL)

NO MATTER WHAT MY WOES AND CARES
TRY KEEP A DOOR ALWAYS OPEN
THOUGH NEGATIVE CAN BE EMOTIONS
I KNOW LORD HEARS ALL MY PRAYERS

OFTEN PROBLEMS COMES IN DOUBLES
BUT HE FIXES ALL THAT'S BROKEN
NO MATTER WHAT MY WOES AND CARES
TRY KEEP A DOOR ALWAYS OPEN

SET EYES ON HIM, HIS LOVE WEAR
KEEP STRONG NO MATTER WHAT HAPPEN
THANK YOU GOD FOR POETRY I PEN
GOD IS WITH ME AND WIPE MY TEARS
NO MATTER WHAT MY WOES AND CARES.

~I LOVE GOD~
(SONNETTE)

LOVE GOD WITH HEART SOUL.
WANT LIVE IN HIS WILL.
LORD GIVES ME A THRILL.
HE MAKES ME FEEL WHOLE.

RESPECT HIM SO TRUE.
GIVE TO ALL FREE WILL.
WITH HIM CAN'T BE BLUE.

*

*

*

~WITH GOD~

(JESUS TEARS)

SO
MANY
THINGS MAKE ME
FEEL SO VERY SAD
SOME DAYS ARE SO HARD
BUT THEN WITH GOD'S
HELP I CAN
GO THRU
THEM

MY
GOD'S THERE
HE'S MY STRENGTH
EACH TIME I PRAY
IN HIM MY HEART TRUST
HE STANDS BY ME
FOREVER
I JUST
KNOW

IN
THE LORD
I CAN REST
AND HAVE PEACE BACK
WHEN I GO TO HIM
NEVER REJECTS
HE LOVES AND
CARES FOR
ME.

TRUST ALL THE WAY~

(MIRRORED REFRAIN)

HE WON'T EVER LEAVE YOU ALONE
HE'S ALWAYS THERE WITH YOU TO STAY
YOU HAVE SO MUCH PAIN AND SORROW
I JUST PRAY FOR YOU EVERY DAY

HIS MERCY EACH DAY YOU WILL SEE
IN THE LORD THERE'S ALWAYS TOMORROW
I JUST PRAY FOR YOU EVERY DAY
YOU HAVE SO MUCH PAIN AND SORROW

JUST THANK HIM FOR ALL THAT HE'S DONE
TRUST TEST HIM AND WALK IN HIS WAY
YOU HAVE SO MUCH PAIN AND SORROW
I JUST PRAY FOR YOU EVERY DAY

COME TO HIM NOW AND JUST REPENT
CARES FOR YOU MORE THAN DOES SPARROW
I JUST PRAY FOR YOU EVERY DAY
YOU HAVE SO MUCH PAIN AND SORROW.

I KNOW WITH GOD CAN ALWAYS WALK
IT'S MY STRENGTH WHEN NEED THE TRUTH TALK
HE GUIDES WITH TRUTH AND DOORS UNLOCK

IN HIM I CAN ALWAYS RELY GROW STRONG MANY INCHES TALL
WITH HIM I CAN JUST REBUILD AND BRING DOWN ANY OLD WALL
WHEN I PRAY AND SEEK IN HIS NAME HE'LL HELP ME NOT TO STALL

IN HIS PRESENCE NONE TO FEAR
HE'S MY COMFORT THAT'S VERY CLEAR
HE WASHES AWAY EACH TEAR

FOR HIM I TAKE STAND
HE'LL RETURN FREE LAND
MANS DAYS ARE LIKE SAND

GOD MADE DAY AND NIGHT
HE'S FULL OF GRACE MIGHT
MAKES BLIND SEE THE LIGHT.

HIS WAY~

(MIRRORED HOURGLASS)

LOVE TRUST HIM AND TEST HIS WAY
HE WON'T LEAVE YOU ALONE
HIS MERCY HE'LL SHOW
WHEN WITH HIM STAY
IN HIS LIGHT
WHEN WALK
WHEN WALK
IN HIS LIGHT
WHEN WITH HIM STAY
HIS MERCY HE'LL SHOW
HE WON'T LEAVE YOU ALONE
LOVE TRUST HIM AND TEST HIS WAY

~MY LORD GOD~
(METAMORPHIC TRANSITION)

NO MATTER WHAT I DID HE ALWAYS SAW ME THRU ALL
EVEN BEFORE I WAS BORN HE'S LOVED ME
SINCE I ACCEPTED THE LORD MY HEART IS FULL OF LOVE AND FREE
HE DIED ON CROSS FOR SINS AND FORGAVE MINE WHEN I REPENTED

WITH JESUS I JUST CAN GO THROUGH ALL
HE GIVES ME HIS LOVE FOREVER I CAN STAND TALL
HIS BLESSINGS EVERYWHERE ARE ALL CLEAR TO SEE
AND IN HIM I HAVE NO FEAR AND CAN ALWAYS BE ME
WITHOUT HIS LOVE I DON'T KNOW WHERE I'D BE NOW
WHEN HAVING A BAD DAY HE'S ALWAYS THERE FOR ME SO
WITH MY GOD THROUGH EVERYTHING I CAN REALLY GO
INSIDE JESUS' LOVE MAKES MY HEART HAPPILY JUST GLOW
HE TEACHES ME ONLY TO LOVE AND ALWAYS TO FORGIVE
LIFE CAN BE SO HARD BUT GOD WANTS ME TO ENJOY IT AND LIVE.

\GOD WILL GIVE YOU AND ME HIS LOVE FOREVER AND EVER
HE'LL RAIN ALL HIS BLESSINGS ON ME AND YOU TOO
AND GRANT HIS FORGIVENESS AND NEVER HE'LL LEAVE ME AND YOU
IN MY HEART AND MIND I WILL ALWAYS WORSHIP MY LORD GOD TOO

~DAY BY DAY~

(SERPENTINE)

DAY BY DAY I PRAISE HIM PRAY TO HIM EACH DAY
WHEN I NEED A FRIEND HE'LL BE THERE AND THATS WHEN
HE SHOWS ALL HIS MERCY TO ME AND THATS ALWAYS
GOD!HE
PRAYING TO HIM GIVES ME STRENGH SO CONTINUE PRAYING
OF NOTHING AT ALL HE WANTS ME TO BE AFRAID OF
LOVE ONLY COMES FROM HIM AND WITH HIM LEARN JUST TO
LOVE
HELP GOD CAN AND HE ALSO WANTS US ALWAYS TO PEOPLE
HELP
PRAY TO MY FATHER GOD FOR LOVE AND PEACE FOR ALL I
JUST PRAY.

~ONE DAY~

(GEORGE'S MIRRORED HOURGLASS)

ONE DAY JESUS WILL RETURN
SITS WITH HIS FATHER NOW
CAME ONCE BEFORE
PROMISED RETURN
I ACCEPT
BELIEVE
BELIEVE
I ACCEPT
PROMISED RETURN
CAME ONCE BEFORE
SITS WITH HIS FATHER NOW

~HOPE FOR A BRAND-NEW DAY~

(TERZA RIMA SONNET)

HOPE FOR A VERY BRAND NEW DAY TOMORROW
AND DONT GIVE IN TO ALL YOUR HURT, YOU'LL BE FINE
JUST BELIEVE THAT ONE DAY THINGS FOR YOU WILL GLOW

PAY ATTENTION WAY YOU LIVE,WALK STRAIGHT THE LINE
YOUR HEART, MINE, HAS ALREADY BEEN HURT SO MUCH
BUT JOYS WAIT AND WITH OTHERS YOU CAN SHARE FINE

MY EYES AND YOURS SHED SO MANY TEARS AND SUCH
WHEN IT COMES TO LOVE BE ALWAYS NICE AND KIND
SHOW WITH HEART THAT YOU CARE JUST REACH AND TOUCH

DON'T LET BAD DAY PUT A FROWN,LEAVE BAD BEHIND
REMEMBER THAT MOST THINGS DONT HAPPEN IN VAIN
THEY SAY THAT IF YOU KEEP JUST LOOKING YOU'LL FIND

SO DON'T STAY LONG UNDER BAD WEATHER AND RAIN
SMILE! ENJOY SUNSHINE WHEN YOU SEE IT AGAIN.

~THE SEED~

(HARRISHAM RHYME)

PLANT A SEED AND EACH DAY FEED IT
THEN WATER IT WITH LOVE EACH DAY
NEXT PRAY TO GOD THAT YOU GROW IT FIT
THE LORD JUST SEND SEEDS YOUR WAY
EARN YOUR WAY,DO YOUR BEST DON'T QUIT
NEW DREAMS AND HOPES FOR THOSE PRAY.

~MEDITATIONS~

(SENRYU SUIT)

SITTING RIGHT HERE NOW
MEDITATING ABOUT LIFE
SOMETIMES NOT EASY

GOD DOES NOT PROMISE
THAT EVERYTHING WILL BE FINE
BUT SAYS HE'LL BE THERE

WHEN WALK IN DARKNESS
HE'LL GUIDE YOU IF YOU LET HIM
AND WILL HOLD YOUR HAND

WHEN SOMETIMES YOU FALL
AND NOTHING MAY SEEM GO RIGHT
JUST GET UP STAND TALL

NOTHING IS PERFECT
THE SKY IS NOT ALWAYS BLUE
SOMETIMES IT IS GRAY

BUT SOON CLOUDS WILL CLEAR
WILL STOP RAINING SEE SUNSHINE
AN RAINBOW APPEAR

~IN HIS DIVINE LOVE~

(HARRISHAM RHYME)

I KNOW THAT NO MATTER WHAT MY TROUBLE

ON HIM I CAN TRUST, FOR HIM MY HEART GLOW

I NEVER DOUBT HE'S WITH ME WHEN STORM COMES

REST ON HIS LOVE, STAY COURSE WITH HIM I KNOW

HEAR PRAYERS,GIVE ME STRENGTH WHEN STRUGGLE

AND IN HIS DIVINE LOVE MY SOUL OVERFLOW.

~OH LORD MY GOD~

(NONET/REVERSED NONET)

OH LORD HELP ME IN MY DAILY WALK
AND IN YOUR NAME JUST LET ME TALK
GUIDE ME SO I CANNOT FALL
I WANT TO HEAR YOUR CALL
HIDE ME FROM MY FOES
AND HELP ME GROW
LET IT SHOW
AND GLOW
SO

OH
LORD GOD
YOU'RE MY ROD
HELP ME TO DO
WHAT IS RIGHT AND TRUE
YOU'RE MY PORT IN ALL STORMS
MY NIGHTS TO DAYS YOU TRANSFORM
WHEN LIFE IS FULL OF GLOOM AND STRIFE
I KNOW YOU'RE ALWAYS THERE IN MY LIFE.

~IN HIM~
(PANTOUM)

FOR GOD MY SOUL THIRSTS IT SO WELL
IN HIM ALWAYS FIND A FRIEND TRUE
HE IS THERE FOR ME I CAN TELL
BECAUSE HE CARES FOR ME, YOU TOO.

IN HIM ALWAYS FIND A FRIEND TRUE
IN HIS LOVE I JUST DO THE WALK
BECAUSE HE CARES FOR ME, YOU TOO
WITH ALL KINDNESS TO PEOPLE TALK.

IN HIS LOVE I JUST DO THE WALK
HE IS THERE FOR ME I CAN TELL
WITH ALL KINDNESS TO PEOPLE TALK
FOR GOD MY SOUL THIRSTS IT SO WELL.

~ENJOY~

(ALOUETTE)

TAKE A MOMENT NOW
TO BREATHE DEEP THAT'S HOW
PAUSE SMELL SOMETIMES THE ROSES
SMELL COFFEE TODAY
SPARE A MINUTE TOO
ENJOY BEFORE DAY CLOSES

JUST SEE MORE AGAIN
SIT BACK RELAX BRAIN
LOOK AT THE BEAUTY AROUND
SO MUCH BEAUTY'S THERE
MANY THINGS TO SHARE
ENJOY ALL GOOD THINGS YOU'VE FOUND.

~A WONDERFUL GIFT~

(DOUBLE TETRACTYS)

LIFE
IS A
GIFT FROM GOD
LIFE CAN BE SHORT
BUT TODAY'S BLESSING 'CAUSE YOU'RE STILL ALIVE.

LIFE IS A MOST WONDERFUL GIFT FROM GOD
AND TODAYS IS YOURS
BE HAPPY
AND NOT
SAD

*

*

*

SALUTATIONS~

(HAIKU SUIT)

THIS MORNING IS GREAT
THE AIRS REFRESHING AND COOL
AUTUMN'S ALMOST HERE

FEELING OF NEWNESS
THERE'S SOME LIGHTNESS AROUND NOW
AND THE BIRDS STILL ROAM

NEW DAYS JUST STARTING
THERE'S SO MUCH TO DO TODAY
SO MANY NEW PLANS

THANK GOD FOR TODAY
THINK OF FRIENDS AND FAMILY
FOR THEM SEND PRAYER

WISH THEM ALL THE BEST
EVERYONE'S IN MY HEART THOUGHTS
GOD BLESS THEM AND YOU

PRAYERS GO TO GOD
I AM SO THANKFUL FOR EACH DAY
THAT HE'S GIVEN ME

DAY BELONGS TO HIM
CREATED ALL THAT IS GOOD
MY GOD IS AWESOME

GREATEST PAINTER
MASTERFUL BRUSHWORKS HE PAINTS
EVERYDAY ALL TIME

MANY THINGS TO PLAN

SOME GREAT HOLIDAYS WILL COME SOON AND I'LL CELEBRATE

*

*

*

~SHINING~

(KYRIELLE SONNET)

STAY FOCUS TILL YOU REACH YOUR GOAL
TAKE IT SLOW AND WATCH FOR YOUR SOUL
DON'T RUSH AND YOU WILL BE JUST FINE
KNOW WITH GOD'S LOVE AND HELP YOU'LL SHINE

STAY FOCUS IN YOUR HEART AND MIND
DO YOUR PART REMEMBER GOD'S KIND
AS HE HAS YOUR HEART IN A SHRINE
KNOW WITH GOD'S LOVE AND HELP YOU'LL SHINE

GOD FOR SURE HAS A PLAN FOR YOU
AND ALWAYS SHOWS ALL HIS LOVE TRUE
IF YOU LET HIM YOU'LL WALK THE LINE
KNOW WITH GOD'S LOVE AND HELP YOU'LL SHINE

STAY FOCUS TILL YOU REACH YOUR GOAL
KNOW WITH GOD'S LOVE AND HELP YOU'LL SHINE.

~DAY BY DAY~

(SERPENTINE)

DAY BY DAY I PRAISE HIM PRAY TO HIM EACH DAY
WHEN I NEED A FRIEND HE'LL BE THERE AND THATS WHEN
HE SHOWS ALL HIS MERCY TO ME AND THATS ALWAYS
GOD!HE
PRAYING TO HIM GIVES ME STRENGH SO CONTINUE PRAYING
OF NOTHING AT ALL HE WANTS ME TO BE AFRAID OF
LOVE ONLY COMES FROM HIM AND WITH HIM LEARN JUST TO
LOVE
HELP GOD CAN AND HE ALSO WANTS US ALWAYS TO PEOPLE
HELP
PRAY TO MY FATHER GOD FOR LOVE AND PEACE FOR ALL I
JUST PRAY.

~VERY HAPPY BIRTHDAY TO YOU~

(MEMENTO)

NICE DAY IS HERE SO JUST SMILE SING
TODAY IT'S YOUR BIRTHDAY
NOT BAD
SO DON'T WORRY ABOUT ANYTHING
HAVE PIECE OF CAKE AND PLAY
BE GLAD!

THIS A VERY SPECIAL TIME FOR YOU
JUST CELEBRATE IT ALL
THE WAY
WITH FAMILY, FRIENDS, TOO
BE HAPPY AND STAND TALL
TODAY.

~FALL~

(ACROSTIC)

F ANTASTIC COLOURS TO VIEW
A UTUMN IS SO SWIFTLY APPROACHING
L IGHT BRIGHT AND COOL, TREES CHANGE
L EAVES TURN TO REDS,YELLOWS AND BROWNS.

*

*

*

~A MOTHER'S LOVE~

(SENRYU SUIT)

GOOD MOMS DO THEIR BEST
RAISE CHILDREN WITH LOTS OF LOVE
TEACH GUIDE THEM THRU LIFE

NOT AN EASY JOB
HARD TO BE A GOOD PARENT
JUST LOVE OUR CHILDREN

NEED TEACH RIGHT FROM WRONG
LET THEM KNOW YOU'RE THERE FOR THEM
SHOW LOVE AND RESPECT

AND TEACH THEM TO CARE
BRING THEM UP KNOWING OF GOD
THAT HONESTY'S GREAT

RAISING CHILD NOT EASY
BUT IS JOB THAT CAN BE DONE
BETTER WITH GODS HELP

ALL THESE THAT I SHARE
HERE IN POEM ONLY MY VIEW
AND WHAT I BELIEVE

NEVER HURT YOUR CHILD
ALWAYS PROTECT HIM OR HER
OF EACH AND ALL HARM

~CHANGES~

(DOUBLE TAKE 6'S 5'S AND 4'S)

PRAY FOR LOVE PEACE TODAY
LOVE COMES FROM LORD SEE
HE WILL SET YOU FREE
HELP YOU EACH SINGLE DAY

HE'LL CHANGE YOUR HEART
AND HOLD YOUR HAND
BE MORE HAPPY
WITH HIM CAN FLY
YOU'LL REJOICE

WITH GOD YOU OBTAIN PEACE
THINGS BETTER YOU KNOW
WHEN TROUBLE STIR SO
WITH HIM YOU CAN WIN RACE

HE'LL CHANGE YOUR HEART
AND HOLD YOUR HAND
SING SONG EACH DAY
PRAISE HIS NAME TOO
HIS TEACHINGS NICE.

~YOU ARE~

(TERZA RIMA)

YOU ARE ALWAYS MY BEST FRIEND AND I LOVE YOU
AND NO MATTER WHAT IN THE FUTURE TAKE PLACE
YOU'LL ALWAYS STAND WITH ME IN EVERYTHING TRUE

YOU'RE THE BEST TO ME YOU ALWAYS FULL OF GRACE
ALL THESE YEARS I CARRY YOU INSIDE MY HEART
THERE'S NO DOUBT THAT YOU FILL EVERY SINGLE SPACE

LIFE WITHOUT YOU WOULDN'T BE SAME, OF ME YOU'RE PART
YOU'RE IN EVERYTHING THAT I DO DAY AND NIGHT
YOU'VE GIVEN ME ALL YOUR LOVE FROM THE VERY START

WITH YOU LORD I CAN'T GO WRONG YOU ARE MY LIGHT
YOU'RE MY BEST FRIEND AND YOU HELP ME SEE THINGS RIGHT.

*

*

*

~FIRST~
(SKELETON KEY)

PUT
GOD**FIRST
IN
ALL THAT
I JUST DO
HE HAS A PLAN
FOR ME AND YOU EACH MAN
FOLLOW YOUR DREAMS AND TAKE A STAND
GONE ARE THE GOOD OLD DAYS AND LOVE NEEDS THE LAND
TODAY THANK HIM WITH ALL MY HEART
HEALS WHEN THINGS FALL APART
FROM ME HE'LL NEVER PART
HEART WITH HIM SINGS
HE BRINGS
HIS LIGHT
SO BRIGHT
HIS LOVE
THE BEST
WITH HIM
CAN BE
JUST ME
ALL SINS
FORGIVES
IN HIM
I'M FREE
BLESSINGS
TO ME
AND YOU
HE SENDS
RIGHT FROM
ABOVE

~IN HIS LOVE~

(THE TREE)

HE
CALLS ME
SHOWS ME LOVE
IN HIM I TRUST
LIFTS ME UP ALWAYS
IN HIS LOVE I CAN GLOW
HE GIVES ME ALL THAT I NEED
IN HIM ONLY GOODNESS I'VE FOUND.
H
E
CALLS ME.

*

*

*

~NO MATTER WHAT~

(DAVEDA'S CASCADE)

SO HAPPY MY SOUL YOU DID SAVE
TO SIN I DON'T HAVE TO BE SLAVE
MY HEART IN GOD I CAN CONFIDE
LORD YOU ARE MY LIGHT AND MY GUIDE

YOU ALWAYS GIVE ME LOVE AND JOY
COMFORT SOUL WHEN I FEEL ANNOY
YOU'LL BE WITH ME BEYOND THE GRAVE
SO HAPPY MY SOUL YOU DID SAVE

NO MATTER WHAT TAKES PLACE EACH DAY
IN HIM I CAN HAVE A FRIEND TOO
NONE SHOULD FEAR,SOUL YOU DID SAVE
TO SIN I DON'T HAVE TO BE SLAVE

I KNOW THAT WITH HIM I WILL SHINE
I DON'T RUSH I WILL BE JUST FINE
WITH HIM I CAN TAKE THINGS IN STRIDE
MY HEART IN GOD I CAN CONFIDE

REMAIN FOCUS IN HEART AND MIND
DO MY PART KNOWING THAT GODS KIND
NOTHING FROM HIM CAN EVER HIDE
LORD YOU ARE MY LIGHT AND MY GUIDE.

~BELIEVER~

HOP-SCOTCH)

TRUST LORD WITH ALL HEART,HE'S BEST FRIEND
HE'LL HELP YOU WHEN YOU NEED HEALING
YOUR BROKEN HEART HE WILL JUST MEND
HE'LL LEAD YOU, WITH HIM START WALKING
WITH GOD NOT ALONE, HELP HE SENDS
READ HIS WORD,PRAY,WITH HIM TIME SPEND
PRAY HIS ANGELS TO YOU HE'LL SEND.

*

*

*

~PRAYING FOR YOU~

(SENRYU SUIT)

I'M PRAYING FOR YOU
YOU HAVE SO MUCH PAIN SORROWS
BUT THERE'S ALWAYS HOPE

IN CHRIST THERE'S TOMORROWS
JUST TRUST HIM AND TEST HIS WAYS
HE NEVER LEAVES YOU

HIS MERCY JUST SHOWS
IN HIM ALL IT IS POSSIBLE
IF YOU SEEK HIS LIGHT

NOW HEART BLEEDS FOR YOU
HOPING THAT YOU FIND YOUR WAY
EACH DAY FOR YOU PRAY

*

*

*

~MAY GOD~

(ANAPHORA)

MAY GOD ALWAYS CARE FOR YOU
MAY GOD KEEP YOU STANDING TALL
MAY GOD WHISPER IN YOUR EARS WORDS OF WISDOM
MAY GOD SHOW YOU WHAT YOU NEED TO KNOW
MAY GOD ALWAYS HAVE AN ANGEL FOR YOU
MAY GOD SEND AN ANGEL BY YOUR SIDE
MAY GOD BE THERE TO CATCH YOU FAST EVERY TIME YOU FALL
MAY GOD GIVE YOU SOMEONE WONDERFUL TO LOVE
MAY GOD TEACH YOU LOVE UNTOLD
MAY GOD GIVE YOU HOPES TO KEEP YOU SAFE AND WARM
MAY GOD GRANT YOU WITH MANY GIFTS AND LONG LIFE
MAY GOD KEEP HIS EYES ALWAYS ON YOU
MAY GOD GUIDE EVERY SINGLE STEP OF YOUR WAY
MAY GOD KEEP YOU FROM EACH AND ALL HARM EACH DAY *
MAY GOD ALWAYS SEND AN ANGEL BESIDE YOU
MAY GOD ALWAYS SPEAK TO YOUR HEART MIND AND SOUL.

~FOR HIM~

(CANDLELIGHT)

FOR HIM HEART SING SONG
IN HIM I CAN BE STRONG
HE LIFTS UP MY SOUL
HE MAKES ME WHOLE
HELPS ME SET GOAL
GIVES ME PEACE
HIS LOVE
I HAVE
INSIDE
AND
HOLD
IT
DEEP
IN
MY
HEART
TODAY AND JUST FOREVER.

~FOCUS~

(THE MINUET)

STAY FOCUS TILL YOU REACH YOUR DREAMS
DREAMS ARE SO GREAT
GREAT JUST TO HAVE
HAVE AND ENJOY

AS YOU DO THIS YOU'LL START TO CLIMB
CLIMB, MAKE MUSIC
MUSIC AND RHYME
RHYME, AND YOU'LL SHINE

REST ASSURED THAT THINGS WILL ALIGN
ALIGN FOR YOU
YOU STAY FOCUS
FOCUS AND DREAM.

*

*

AUTHOR'S NOTES: THIS IS MY OWN STYLE.

~BELIEVE~

(CARPE DIEM)

ALWAYS JUST BELIEVE IN YOURSELF
AND DOING GOOD MY FRIEND
BE POSITIVE
JUST SMILE
KEEP NICE ATTITUDE WITH ALL AROUND YOU

JUST SMILE
AND BE HAPPY
BRING HIS COMFORT AND PEACE
SHOW GOOD WILL AND SHARE HIS LOVE
BE THE BEST PERSON YOU CAN BE ALL TIME.

*

*

~CELEBRATE LIFE~

(DEE'S FIVE-SEVEN-TEN)

LET'S CELEBRATE LIFE
PUSH BACK ALL THE STRIFE
WATCH THE CLOCK TICKING BY FAST
DON'T THROW LIFE AWAY
CAST YOUR CARES TODAY
GIVE THEM TO GOD, HIS JOY LAST

THANK THE LORD RIGHT NOW
TIME WON'T WAIT THAT'S HOW
THANK HIM FOR ALL THAT YOU HAVE
ENJOY LIFE, HAVE HOPE
WITH GOD YOU CAN COPE
THRU HIS SON ALL HE CAN SAVE

GOODNESS IN HIM FIND
OPEN YOUR HEART, MIND
THERE'S STILL LOVE, LISTEN TO HEART
SEE LIGHT, DON'T BE BLIND
SHOW YOU CARE AND MIND
DON'T LET FOLKS RIP HEART APART

CELEBRATE LIFE OPEN YOUR HEART WIDE
REGAIN LOST DREAMS,CLIMB MOUNTAIN
REACH OUT TO GOD AND TOUCH EACH SOUL YOU CAN
PRAY GOD FOR ALL MEN'S SINS, STAINS.

~PRAY~

(THE MINUET)

PRAY FOR ALL THE LOST OF THIS WORLD
WORLD NEEDS PRAYERS
PRAYERS AND GOD
GOD CAN SAVE ALL

THE LOST AND CONFUSED TODAY
TODAY IN LIFE
LIFE HE CAN CHANGE
CHANGE ALSO HEART

YOU NEED TO COME TO HIM,REPENT
REPENT RIGHT THERE
THERE, THEN JUST PRAY
PRAY FOR THE LOST

THE " MINUET" IS A POETRY STYLE WAS CREATED BY DORIAN PETERSEN POTTER ON MARCH,3,2012.

~ONLY THE BEST~

(TRINE)

SO MANY THINGS ARE JUST A MYTH
BUT I'VE LEARNED TO LIVE BY FAITH.

I DONT REALLY CARE WHAT THE WORLD SAYS
BECAUSE GOD CAN SEE ME THROUGH ANYWAY.

IN JESUS MY WHOLE LIFE I INVEST
WITH HIM I CAN PASS EVERY SINGLE TEST.

I'VE CHOSEN TO PUT IN GOD MY TRUST AND FAITH
SO EVERY DAY TO HIM I WILL ALWAYS PRAY
I JUST KNOW THAT HE WANTS FOR ME AND YOU ONLY THE
BEST.

*

*

*

~VESSEL OF LIGHT~

(VESSEL OF LIGHT)

OH
CHRIST
MY LORD
LOVE YOU SO
MORE THAN I CAN
EVER SAY WITH WORDS
THANKS FOR SAVING
SOUL FROM HELL
THANKS FOR
ALL

THANKS FOR ALL YOU'VE DONE
YOU ARE REALLY LIGHT OF THIS WORLD
YOU'VE TAUGHT ME HOW TO CLIMB MOUNTAIN
SHOWN ME THAT WITH YOU NOTHING IS IMPOSSIBLE
THAT WITH YOU BY MY SIDE I HAVE NOTHING TO FEAR
YOU'RE ALWAYS THERE TO PICK ME UP WHEN I FALL
YOU KNOW WHAT'S IN MY HEART,FROM YOU I CAN'T HIDE
WHEN I CRY YOU'RE THERE TO WIPE ALL MY TEARS
WHEN I AM SAD AND LONELY YOU'RE THERE WITH ME
I KNOW FOR SURE IN YOU I CAN ALWAYS TRUST
WHEN IN NEED I JUST PRAY AND YOU LISTEN
YOU'RE FULL OF LOVE AND COMPASSION
YOU BRING ME LOVE AND PEACE
YOU'VE DELIVERED MY SOUL
WITH YOU I HAVE IT ALL.

*

~EMBRACE LIFE~

(QUATERN)

EMBRACE YOUR LIFE NO MATTER WHAT.
START WITH HEARTFUL OF LOVE AND HOPES.
NEVER LET YESTERDAY ROB YOUR DREAMS.
LOOK AT THIS DAY WITH BRAND-NEW EYES.

THE BEST FOR YOU MIGHT STILL TO COME.
EMBRACE YOUR LIFE NO MATTER WHAT.
LISTEN TO THE BEAT OF YOUR HEART.
NOTHINGS OVER TILL GOD SAYS SO.

EMBRACE DAY WITH ALL UPS AND DOWNS.
CLIMBING TO TOP OF MOUNTAINS HARD.
EMBRACE YOUR LIFE NO MATTER WHAT.
THERE'S LIGHT AT END OF DARK TUNNEL.

NOTHING STAYS THE SAME IN THIS LIFE.
BUT THERE'S ALWAYS GOD LOVE DREAMS HOPE.
PRAY BE STRONG WHEN THINGS DON'T LOOK GOOD.
EMBRACE YOUR LIFE NO MATTER WHAT.

~HE SEES IT ALL~

(TRITINA)

IT DOESN'T MATTER WHAT YOU MAY THINK.
GOD SEES ME AND HE SEES YOU TOO.
YOU CAN BE CERTAIN HE SEES ALL.

HE GIVES WHAT WE NEED, AND THAT'S ALL.
HE LOVES YOU MORE THAN YOU MAY THINK.
WHEN TROUBLED YOU CAN GO TO HIM TOO.

HE'S THERE WHEN YOU NEED A FRIEND TOO.
WITH HIM, WE SHOULD NOT FEAR AT ALL.
HE'S CLOSER TO YOU THAN YOU THINK.

GOD THINKS OF US TOO AND THAT'S ALL.

~HE'S ALWAYS THERE FOR ME~

(HERALD ANGEL)

IF
I CALL
HIM HE'S
ALWAYS
WITH ME
IN HIM I DO HAVE THE BEST FRIEND THAT I COULD EVER
MEET.WITHOUT HIM I'D BE LOST
JESUS IS HIS NAME AND WHEN I'M BLUE HE LIFTS MY SPIRIT
AND GIVES ME PEACE
WITH HIM BY MY SIDE I SHOULD NO FEAR ANYTHING 'CAUSE
HE CARES FOR ME
HE'S THE BEST FRIEND THAT ANYONE COULD EVER HAVE IN
THEIR LIFE
HE LIFTS ME UP
HE PROTECTS ME
HE MAKES ME STRONG
WHEN THINGS ARE WRONG
WITH HIM I CAN
BE JUST MYSELF
WITH HIM PASS TEST
HE LOVES ME BEST
WITH HIM I WANT
TO BE EACH DAY
BECAUSE IS MY
BEST FRIEND FOR SURE
I'M SO HAPPY
HE'S WITH ME EACH
DAY AND ALL NIGHT
GOD'S MY DELIGHT.

~WITHOUT GOD

(QUATERN)

PRESSURES IN LIFE STRONG AND MANY.
THE DEVIL JUST WANT TO DESTROY.
HE'LL DO THIS ONLY IF ALLOWED.
BUT WITH GOD HE HAS NO POWER.

WORLD BEAUTIFUL BUT FILL'D OF SIN.
PRESSURES IN LIFE STRONG AND MANY.
WHAT'S GOOD TO HAVE ALL WITHOUT GOD?
THERE'S LACK OF LOVE AND COMPASSION.

NOTHING IN THIS WORLD'S FOREVER.
TRY TO LIVE MY LIFE BEST I CAN.
PRESSURES IN LIFE STRONG AND MANY.
I MAY NOT HAVE FRIENDS BUT HAVE GOD.

GOD WATCHES MY BACK ALL THE TIME.
WITH HIM I HAVE MY LIFE AND MORE.
WITHOUT GOD I'D BEEN GONE AND LOST.
PRESSURES IN LIFE STRONG AND MANY.

~LIVING LIFE~

(QUATERN)

EXPERIENCES EARN'D FROM LIVING LIFE.
YOU CAN READ BUT ARE YOU LEARNING?
EVERYTHING IN LIFE HAS PRICE TAG.
YOU CAN'T PASS TESTS WITHOUT FIRE.

DON'T LOOK OUT TOO MUCH SEE INSIDE.
EXPERIENCES EARN'D FROM LIVING LIFE.
WHEN LIFE THROW YOU ROCKS MAKE A SOUP.
TURN PAGE OF BOOK WHEN DONE GO NEXT.

NOTHING IN THIS LIFE LAST FOREVER.
LOOK 'ROUND TWICE DO YOU SEE THINGS SAME?
EXPERIENCES EARN'D FROM LIVING LIFE.
MAKE PEACE WITH SELF DON'T LOOK BACK.

LIFE'S SCHOOL OF LEARNING EVERYDAY.
ARE YOU LEARNING FROM YOUR MISTAKES?
WHEN LIFE HAND YOU LEMONS MAKE JUICE.
EXPERIENCES EARN'D FROM LIVING LIFE.

OF ALL~

(CROSS OF SALVATION)

WITH GOD STAND TALL
HE HELPS IN ALL
GOD IS WITH ME
HE'S MY BEST FRIEND
BROKEN HEART MENDS
GOD IS THE BEST
HELPS ME PASS TESTS
SIN WITH HIM FLEES
GOD IS ALWAYS WITH ME EVERYDAY WHEN I FALL
WITH FAITH IN HIM I KNOW I CAN CONQUER IT ALL
JESUS,GOD'S BELOVED SON TEACHES ABOUT LOVE I KNOW
IN GOOD TIMES AND BAD TIMES HE GUIDES AND HELPS ME GROW
KNOWING JESUS MAKES STRONG
HIS LOVE FOR ME JUST GLOWS
WITH JESUS I CAN'T FALL
WITH HIM I ENDURE ALL
HAPPY THAT I KNOW HIM
HIS LOVE WILL NEVER DIM
HE TELLS ALL GOOD I KNOW
GOES WITH ME WHERE I GO
HELPS ME PASS TESTS
HIS LOVE THE BEST
IN GOD CAN REST

~LIFE~

(TRITINA)

LEARNING NEW THINGS EVERYDAY IS FUN.
THERE'S ALWAYS SOMETHING NEW TO LEARN.
LIFE'S NOT EASY ALL TIME I KNOW.

BUT IT'S NOT JUST HARD NEITHER I KNOW.
THERE ARE SOME THINGS THAT CAN BE FUN.
SOME THINGS CAN BE SO HARD TO LEARN.

MANY LESSONS IN LIFE TO LEARN.
LIFE CAN MAKE US GROW QUICK WE KNOW.
SO MUCH PAIN SOMETIMES, THATS NOT FUN.

LIFE CAN BE FUN, LEARN FROM IT, KNOW.

*

*

*

~PRESS FORWARD~

(FREE STYLE)

KEEP CLIMBING THE MOUNTAIN
TILL YOU MAKE IT RIGHT TO THE TOP.
BELIEVE THAT YOU CAN MAKE IT THRU
AND JUST NEVER GIVE UP OR STOP.

YOU CAN ACCOMPLISH ANYTHING
YOU DESIRE IN YOUR HEART TO DO.
JUST BELIEVE IT WITH ALL YOUR MIGHT
AND THEN YOU WILL MAKE IT THRU.

DON'T LOOK BACK BUT PRESS FORWARD.
DON'T STOP AND GIVE UP ALONG THE WAY.
DON'T BE AFRAID TO STUMBLE AND FALL SOMETIMES.
JUST FOCUS YOUR EYES ON JESUS AND PRAY.

HE'S RIGHT THERE WITH YOU TODAY AND EVERY DAY.
BECAUSE GOD LOVES YOU AND CARES FOR YOU HE SAYS.

*

*

*

WITH HIM I HAVE MORE~

(OCTAZ-RHYME)

HE PROVIDES
WITH HIM I HAVE MORE
IN HIS LOVE AND CARE I JUST SOAR
HE PROVIDES HEALING TO MY BROKEN HEART
FROM HIM MY HEART WILL NOT PART
WITH HIM ALL I SHARE
I CAN BEAR AND
CONFIDE.

*

*

*

~LOVE IS~

(RICTAMETER)

LOVE IS
SO WONDERFUL.
THE MOST BEAUTIFUL THING
ANYONE CAN REALLY HAVE.
LOVE IS GIVEN UNCONDITIONALLY.
MANY FOLKS SADLY DON'T HAVE LOVE.
THEY JUST GO WITHOUT IT.
SO KIND AND NICE
LOVE IS.

TRUE LOVE
IS REALLY
VERY KIND,NICE,PATIENT.
DOESN'T PUFFS UP AND WANTS TO HURT YOU.
WHEN SOMEONE LOVES YOU THEY JUST WANT TO HELP.
LOVE'S GIVING NOT JUST RECEIVING.
IT IS CARING AND THE
LOVE FROM GOD IS
TRUE LOVE.

*

*

~DAY BY DAY~

(QUATERN)

DAY BY DAY WITH GOD MAKE MY WAY.
WITH COURAGE I NEED TO DO THIS.
I'LL NEVER QUIT NO MATTER WHAT.
I WILL HOLD MY HEAD HIGH ALL TIME.

RISE WALK THRU ALL IN SPITE OF WRONGS.
DAY BY DAY WITH GOD MAKE MY WAY.
IN HEART WANT TO FOLLOW HIS PLAN.
THAT CAN BE DONE I KNOW CAN BE.

PROCEED WITH CARE WITH SONG IN HEART.
WITHIN IT I LISTEN HIS VOICE.
DAY BY DAY WITH GOD MAKE MY WAY.
WITH HIM BESIDE ACCOMPLISH THIS.

SOMETIMES I HAVE LOTS IN MY PLATE.
ALWAYS SET GOALS WHERE BELONG TO.
WITH GOD AND FAITH CONQUER FEAR ALL.
DAY BY DAY WITH GOD MAKE MY WAY.

*

*

~FROM YOU LORD~

(THE TREE)

FROM
YOU LORD
GAIN MY STRENGTH
I TRUST IN YOU
WITH YOU HAVE A HOME
IN YOUR LOVE TRULY GLOW
TO YOU I COME IN PRAYER
HELP ME EVERYDAY NOT TO STRAY
F
R
O
M
YOU LORD.

~FAR FROM HOME~
(BLESSED CROSS)

GOD CAN PROTECT US FROM ANY HARM
HAVING HIM BETTER THAN ANY CHARM
HIS WORD SAYS WE'RE NEVER ALONE
NO MATTER CLOSE OR FAR FROM HOME.

NOBODY KNOWS WHEN OUR TIME ON EARTH WILL JUST END
WON'T YOU COME TO HIM TODAY AS YOU ARE MY FRIEND
JUST ACCEPT HIS SALVATION AS TO HIM YOU PRAY
JESUS CAN'T AND WON'T FORCE YOU IN ANY WHICH WAY.

ONCE YOU REPENT INVITE HIM IN
RECEIVE HIS GIFT HE'LL WASH YOUR SIN
HE OFFERS SALVATION TO ALL
MAKE SURE YOU HEED HIS LOVING CALL.

NO ONE ELSE CAN DO THIS BUT YOU
GOD WILL HELP YOU IN ALL YOU DO
FAR FROM HOME BUT NOT FROM FATHER
IF YOU DON'T HAVE HIM LIFE'S HARDER.

GOD CAN PROTECT US FROM ANY HARM
ONCE YOU REPENT INVITE HIM IN
NO ONE ELSE CAN DO THIS BUT YOU
HAVING HIM IS BETTER THAN ANY CHARM
RECEIVE HIS GIFT HE'LL WASH YOUR SIN
GOD WILL HELP YOU IN ALL YOU DO.

~TESTING TIMES~

(CROSS OF SALVATION)

TESTING TIME HARD
IT HURTS MY HEART
I COME TO YOU
CAN'T STAND THIS PAIN
CONSUMES MY SOUL
NO LONGER SEE
I'M TOO CONFUSED
I WANT YOU LORD

BUT IN ALL THESE TESTING TIME I KNOW THAT YOU'RE HERE
YOU'RE IN CONTROL OF EVERYTHING AND YOU ARE NEAR
I'LL NEVER REBEL AGAINST YOU OR DOUBT YOUR WILL
I COME TO YOU WITH PRAISES AND THANKSGIVING STILL

YOUR WILL BE DONE TODAY
MY LIFE BELONGS TO YOU
GIVE ME UNDERSTANDING
FILL SOUL WITH PEACE AND LOVE
SEND YOUR GRACE FROM ABOVE
I TRUST YOU FOREVER
MAKE ME SEE THINGS BETTER
PLEASE ACCEPT MY LETTER

ANSWER PRAYER
YOU'RE MY FATHER
YOU KNOW BETTER

~ETERNALLY~

(QUATERN)

WE CAN'T HELP BUT LOOK AT THE CLOCK
IT'S TIME TO MOVE ON FOR THE DAY
DO MANY THINGS 'ROUND HERE AND THERE
CAUSE TIME NEVER STOPS FOR ME,YOU

SINCE WE WAKE UP TILL WE GO SLEEP
WE CAN'T HELP BUT LOOK AT THE CLOCK
TIME ADVANCES AND ENDLESSLY SO
DESIGNED BY GOD AND ETERNALLY

WE NEED TO GET OUR BREATH SOMETIMES
ON EARTH ALL ENDS BUT SOUL I KNOW
WE CAN'T HELP BUT LOOK AT THE CLOCK
THOSE LEFT STILL DEAL WITH TIME,THAT'S RIGHT

TIME TICK AND TOCK THE CLOCKS ALL TIME
TAKE IT EASY IN ALL YOU DO
REMEMBER TAKE TIME FOR REST TOO
WE CAN'T HELP BUT LOOK AT THE CLOCK.

FRIEND~

(PANTOUM)

NO DOUBT THAT JESUS IS MY FRIEND
IN EVERYTHING CAN COUNT ON HIM
HOPE AND PEACE TO MY SOUL HE SEND
HIS LOVE IS NEVER RUDE OR DIM.

IN EVERYTHING CAN COUNT ON HIM
WHEN PEOPLE AROUND LET ME DOWN
HIS LOVE IS NEVER RUDE OR DIM
IN HIM A BEST FRIEND I HAVE FOUND.

WHEN PEOPLE AROUND LET ME DOWN
PEACE AND HOPE TO MY SOUL HE SEND
IN HIM A BEST FRIEND I HAVE FOUND
NO DOUBT THAT JESUS IS MY FRIEND.

*

*

*

About the Author

Dorian Petersen Potter has been writing poetry for most of her life. Her poetry has been published in many anthologies and poetry collections all over the world. Her poetry today can be found in many places in the internet and in several of her poetry pages too.

Dorian's personal websites:

"Poetic Dreams"

http://www.PoetryPoem.com/ladydp2000

and

http://publishing with passion.com/dorianpetersenpotter.html

www.ingramcontent.com/pod-product-compliance
Ingram Content Group UK Ltd.
Pitfield, Milton Keynes, MK11 3LW, UK
UKHW041919190726
13854UKWH00003B/1339